# 13 Colonies

RHODE ISLAND

## *13 Colonies*

# RHODE ISLAND

## THE HISTORY OF RHODE ISLAND COLONY, 1636–1776

ROBERTA WIENER AND JAMES R. ARNOLD

Raintree

Chicago, Illinois

For information, address the publisher:
Raintree, 100 N. LaSalle, Suite 1200, Chicago, IL 60602

Printed and bound in China

08 07 06 05 04
10 9 8 7 6 5 4 3 2 1

Library of Congress Cataloging-in-Publication Data
Wiener, Roberta, 1952-
  Rhode Island / Roberta Wiener and James R. Arnold.
     p. cm. -- (13 colonies)
Summary: Examines the early colonization of Rhode Island, discussing the struggles the colonists went through, their government, daily lives, and more.
Includes bibliographical references and index.
  ISBN 0-7398-6887-X (lib. bdg.) -- ISBN 1-4109-0311-7 (pbk.)
  1. Rhode Island--History--Colonial period, ca. 1600-1775--Juvenile literature. [1. Rhode Island--History--Colonial period, ca. 1600-1775.]
I. Arnold, James R. II. Title.  III. Series: Wiener, Roberta, 1952-
13 colonies.
  F82.W59 2004
  974.5'01--DC22
                            2003018475

Title page picture: An early view of the college, built in Providence in 1770, that eventually became Brown University.

Opposite: The prosperous and growing town of Newport around 1730

The authors wish to thank Walter Kossmann, whose knowledge, patience, and ability to ask all the right questions have made this a better series.

Picture Acknowledgments

Courtesy American Antiquarian Society: 38 Authors: 51 William Cullen Bryant, et. al., *Scribner's Popular History of the United States*, 1896: 7, 10-11, 20 bottom Colonial Williamsburg Foundation: 6, 32-33, 37 right, 45, 52 top ET Archives: 27 *Howard Pyle's Book of the American Spirit*, 1923: 19, 26, 30, 32 Independence National Historical Park: 57 top right and bottom Library Company of Philadelphia: 18 Library of Congress: 15, 16, 24-25, 28, 29, 37 left, 39, 42, 43 bottom, 48 bottom, 49, 52 bottom, 54, 57 top left National Archives: 34-35 Courtesy of the Rhode Island Historical Society: Cover and 53 (RHi X5 10), title page and 58-59 (RHi X5 172), 5 and 40-41 (RHi X3 2287), 9 (RHi X3 6632), 13 (RHi X4 92), 14 top (RHi X3 6135), 14 bottom (RHi X4 195), 17 (RHi X4 22), 20 top (RHi X3 6091), 22 (RHi X3 774), 23, 36 (RHi X3 855), 43 top (RHi X5 17), 44 (photographer John T. Hopf, RHi X3 2768), 46-47 (RHi X42 72), 48 top (RHi X4 187), 50 (RHi X5 84), 55 (RHi X3 1277), 56 (RHi X3 575)

# Contents

# PROLOGUE: THE WORLD IN 1636

In the year 1636, Roger Williams and his followers—forced out of Massachusetts—found a safe haven at Providence Plantation, part of the present-day state of Rhode Island. For Europeans, both the territory of the known world and the ways of believing in Christianity were expanding as never before. Perhaps it was inevitable that new ways of religious belief would take root in new lands.

Long ago, Europe had begun to explore the wider world during the Renaissance, a 150-year period of invention and discovery beginning during the 1400s. Advances in navigation and the building of better sailing ships allowed longer voyages. So began the Age of Exploration, with great sailors from Portugal, Spain, Italy, the Netherlands, France, and England sailing into uncharted waters. The explorers eventually reached Africa, India, the Pacific Ocean, China, Japan, and finally Australia. They encountered kingdoms and civilizations that had existed for centuries.

The voyages from Europe to these distant shores went around Africa. This made the trip long and dangerous. So, European explorers began to sail westward in search of shortcuts. In 1492, the explorer Christopher Columbus landed on an island on the far side of the Atlantic Ocean

A map shows how Europeans saw the world around 1570.

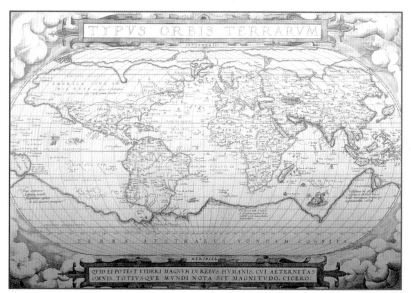

In 1524 the explorer Giovanni da Verrazano compared the size of Block Island to the Mediterranean island of Rhodes. His comparison later led to the entire colony being named Rhode Island. Verrazano's ship is shown here anchored in Narragansett Bay.

and claimed it for Spain. He thought he had actually sailed all the way around the world and come to an island near India. Years of exploration by numerous sailors passed before the people of Europe realized that Columbus had been the first European of their era to set foot in a land unknown to them. They called this land the New World, although it was not new to the people who lived there. After Columbus, Amerigo Vespucci claimed to have reached the New World. Whether he actually did or not, in 1507 a mapmaker put his name on a map, and the New World became America, or the Americas. Still looking for a shortcut to the riches of Asia, European explorers continued to sail to North and South America. They began to claim large pieces of these continents for their own nations.

The first English ship to cross the Atlantic Ocean was commanded by the Italian-born John Cabot in 1497. Cabot's exploration of the eastern coast of Canada formed the basis for all of England's future claims to American colonies.

A succession of explorers subsequently made landfall on the eastern coast of North America, and several of them explored the coast of Rhode Island. The Italian sailor, Giovanni da Verrazano, commanded a French expedition in 1524 and explored and charted the coast from the Carolinas to Maine. Verrazano sailed into Narragansett Bay, and he and his crew spent two weeks exploring the bay. They found two Native American tribes, the Narragansetts and the Wampanoags, living on opposite sides of the bay. The Native Americans were fighting with one another over control of some of the islands in the bay. Verrazano returned to Europe to report to his sponsors in France that the bay had an excellent natural harbor. No one paid any attention. The little-known Esteban Gomez charted a portion of the New England coast for Spain the following year.

In the meantime, Walter Raleigh sponsored expeditions to America and claimed for England a large expanse of land he called Virginia. The disappearance of his colonists from Roanoke Island some time after 1587 remains a mystery.

In 1602, Englishman Bartholomew Gosnold set sail to New England hoping to start a colony. After successfully landing on the Massachusetts coast, Gosnold and his men decided they did not have enough food to survive, so they returned to England with a ship full of furs, logs, and **sassafras** roots. Gosnold was followed in 1603 by English trader Martin Pring, also in search of sassafras and other trade goods. French explorer Samuel de Champlain then spent two years charting the New England coast and searching out a site for a French colony, but hard winters and French politics conspired to defeat the effort.

Members of the Virginia Company, which had founded the colony at Jamestown, at the same time sponsored a New England colony on the coast of Maine. This colony failed because, after one winter, the settlers found life too harsh. The unsuccessful colonists returned to England in 1608. In 1614 Adriaen Block, of the Netherlands, mapped the Rhode Island coast. Modern-day Block Island was named after him. Former Virginia colonist, Captain John Smith, explored and mapped the coast of New England in 1614, and his description kept interest in the area alive. But New England, with its cold northern winters, needed settlers with a special kind of endurance to found a lasting colony. The Pilgrims and **Puritans** were the first European settlers to show such endurance.

SASSAFRAS: TYPE OF TREE WHOSE BARK IS USED FOR FLAVORING AND MEDICINAL PURPOSES

PURITANS: PROTESTANTS WHO WANTED THE CHURCH OF ENGLAND TO PRACTICE A MORE "PURE" FORM OF CHRISTIANITY

Europe was no stranger to religious strife when English Christians began looking for a religious haven in America. For centuries in western Europe, Christianity and Roman Catholicism had been one and the same, with all Christians paying allegiance to the Pope, who ruled from Rome. But in 1517 Martin Luther, a German monk, protested against some of the actions of the Roman Catholic church, and so began the **Protestant** Reformation. In 1534 the English king Henry VIII, took advantage of the Protestant Reformation. The Pope would not grant him a divorce, so he formed the Church of England and declared himself its head. The Church of England, also called the **Anglican** Church, became a Protestant church, independent of the Pope, but still Christian.

Then, in 1554, Queen Mary restored Catholicism as the official religion of England. She executed more than 250 people who had continued practicing Protestantism, and for this reason people called her "Bloody Mary." Five years later, Queen Elizabeth I restored the Church of England. Under her rule, and that of the next two kings, Catholicism was outlawed, and those who continued to practice it faced arrest. Even under Protestant rule, however, many English Protestants grew dissatisfied with the Church of England. Among them were the Pilgrims and the Puritans who came to New England beginning in 1620. As the Plymouth and Massachusetts Bay colonies grew, attracting people fleeing the religious intolerance of England, some of these people in turn were forced to flee the intolerance of Massachusetts.

In 1614 the Dutch sailor, Adriaen Block, explored the Rhode Island coast, giving his name to modern-day Block Island.

PROTESTANT: ANY CHRISTIAN CHURCH THAT HAS BROKEN FROM AWAY FROM ROMAN CATHOLIC OR EASTERN ORTHODOX CONTROL

ANGLICAN: CHURCH OF ENGLAND, A PROTESTANT CHURCH AND THE STATE CHURCH OF ENGLAND

# I.
# RHODE ISLAND IN 1636

At the end of the Ice Age, the retreat of the **glaciers** formed a network of channels and coves along what became Rhode Island's coast. The Atlantic Ocean flowed into this network to create Narragansett Bay. At the place where the bay opened to the ocean, nature created a fine natural harbor. It was near the ocean yet sheltered from storms, and deep enough for sailing ships to anchor there.

Edible fish, a variety of shellfish, and lobsters thrived in the bay. There were also many islands, including Aquidneck—the first place to be called Rhode Island by the English colonists—that proved important to the development of agriculture. All around the bay were large cleared fields where Native Americans had once grown crops. Thick grass had taken over the abandoned fields. The white settlers eventually used these old fields to feed their livestock.

Inland, the glaciers' retreat left hills and ponds. Rivers and streams carved valleys leading to the ocean. The three

EXPORT: TO SEND
MERCHANDISE OUT OF THE
COUNTRY FOR SALE;
MERCHANDISE SENT OUT
OF THE COUNTRY

most important rivers are the Blackstone, Pawtuxet, and Pawcatuck. The eastern part of Rhode Island is the Coastal Lowlands. Inland, the western portion of Rhode Island rises gradually to become part of the New England Upland. This area of rolling hills includes Rhode Island's highest point, Jerimoth Hill, at 812 feet (247 meters) above sea level. Towering forests once covered most of the inland parts of Rhode Island. English settlers would one day use these forests to build homes and ships and to make wood products for **export**.

Because of the influence of the nearby ocean, Rhode Island has a milder climate than neighboring states. However, Rhode Island features remarkably variable weather. Hurricanes and tropical storms periodically strike the state and severe winter ice and snow storms are not uncommon.

An English explorer reported to the Puritans that "The country on the west of the Bay of Narragansett is all [level] for many miles, but very stony, and full of Indians."

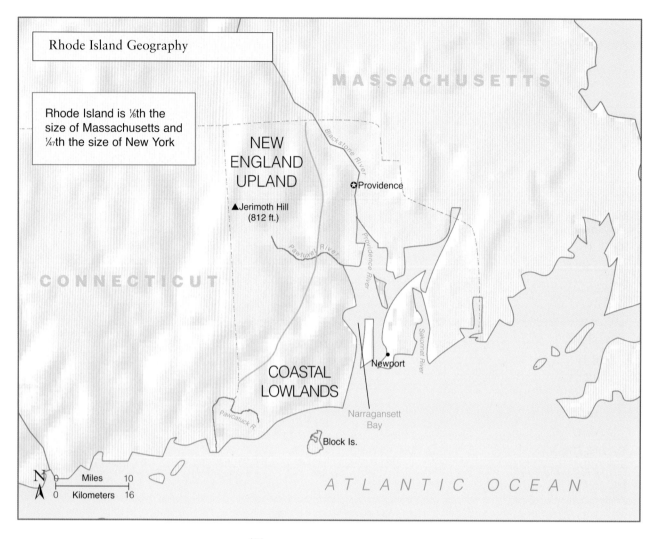

Rhode Island Geography

Rhode Island is ⅛th the size of Massachusetts and ¼₇th the size of New York

MASSACHUSETTS

NEW ENGLAND UPLAND

Blackstone River

⛢Providence

▲Jerimoth Hill (812 ft.)

Pawtuxet River

Providence River

CONNECTICUT

COASTAL LOWLANDS

Sakonnet River

•Newport

Pawcatuck R.

Narragansett Bay

Block Is.

N

| 0 | Miles | 10 |
| 0 | Kilometers | 16 |

ATLANTIC OCEAN

## THE NATIVE PEOPLES

The Narragansett people occupied most of Rhode Island. They belonged to the Algonquian linguistic family. The name Narragansett means "people of the small point." In the early 1600s there were probably about 5,000 Narragansett people, including a related people, the Niantic. The Narragansetts were the most powerful tribe of southern New England. They were successful warriors who drove rival Native Americans, including the Wampanoags of Massachusetts, from the territory that eventually became the state of Rhode Island. Small bands of Nipmuc and Pequot people had also lived in Rhode Island until the Narragansetts drove them from their land in the years prior to English settlement.

The Narragansetts were divided among several local bands, each led by a chief called a sachem. The sachems made the weighty decisions regarding alliances and war or peace. The Native Americans moved with the seasons, settling into small villages of wigwams, houses built of poles covered with bark or animal skins. In spring they moved to coastal areas where the men cleared fields using hatchets to slash through the bark and kill the trees, and fire to burn away the underbrush. The men hunted and fished while the women became farmers for the season, planting corn, squash, and beans between the tree stumps. They fertilized their crops with fish. Men were in charge of growing tobacco.

After the harvest in the early autumn, the women took down the wigwams and the people moved inland to find winter quarters. The women then rebuilt the wigwams. During the winter, the Native Americans mostly ate meat. They were skilled at making canoes, which they used to travel on the rivers.

A great **epidemic** had swept through the Native Americans

EPIDEMIC: WIDESPREAD
OUTBREAK OF CONTAGIOUS
DISEASE

The Narragansett sachem, or leader, Canonicus

of the New England coast in 1617, possibly caught from European explorers. The epidemic missed the Narragansetts. In fact, bands of neighboring Native Americans who escaped the epidemic fled their homes to live with the Narragansetts. However, in 1633 a smallpox epidemic killed about 700 Narragansetts.

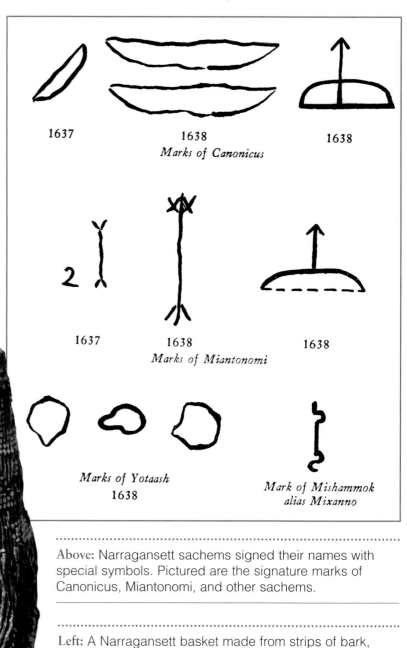

1637

1638
*Marks of Canonicus*

1638

1637

1638
*Marks of Miantonomi*

1638

*Marks of Yotaash*
1638

*Mark of Mishammok
alias Mixanno*

**Above:** Narragansett sachems signed their names with special symbols. Pictured are the signature marks of Canonicus, Miantonomi, and other sachems.

**Left:** A Narragansett basket made from strips of bark, around 1675.

## 2.
# THE ARRIVAL OF THE EUROPEANS

The Pilgrims came to Massachusetts in 1620 and established Plymouth Colony. During the colony's early years, the Pilgrims were allied with the Wampanoags. The Narragansett Indians considered any ally of their foe to be an enemy. However, this hostile attitude did not lead to war between the English colonists and the Narragansetts.

The Puritans formed a new colony, Massachusetts Bay Colony, in 1629. During the next years, increasing numbers of Puritans entered Massachusetts. This buildup alarmed the Narragansett leaders. However, the Narragansetts also had powerful foes among the neighboring Native American people. For this reason, two Narragansett leaders, Canonicus and Miantonomi, agreed to allow Roger Williams to occupy land at the head of Narragansett Bay. They thought that the English colonists would protect them from Wampanoag attacks. Meanwhile, the Narragansetts would be able to fight their other enemies, the Pequots and the Mohegans, who lived to the west in Connecticut.

## RELIGIOUS FREEDOM LEADS TO SETTLEMENT

Roger Williams arrived in Boston in 1631. He was a **radical** religious thinker who believed that the Puritans

RADICAL: HOLDING BELIEFS THAT ARE EXTREMELY DIFFERENT FROM THOSE OF THE MAJORITY; BELIEVING IN THE NEED FOR MAJOR CHANGES IN SOCIETY

Roger Williams wrote, "I, having made covenants of peaceable neighborhood with all the sachems and natives round about us, and having a sense of God's merciful providence unto me in my distress, called the place Providence; I desired it be for a shelter for persons distressed of conscience."

# The Life of Roger Williams

Roger Williams was born in London at an unknown date but probably in 1603. His father was a merchant. Roger received an education at Cambridge, one of England's elite universities. He was a deep religious thinker whose ideas of the correct way to practice religion separated him from almost everyone else. In order to pursue his religious ideas, Williams went to Boston in 1631.

He could not get along with the Puritans who controlled religious life in the Massachusetts Bay Colony. So, the next year Williams moved to Plymouth Colony where the Pilgrims held different religious ideas. Williams also ran into conflict with the leaders of Plymouth Colony. He insisted that they had no right to the land because the Native Americans already owned it.

In 1634 Williams returned to Massachusetts Bay Colony where he served as pastor to the church in Salem. Again he stirred up trouble. Not only did he say that the colonists had no right to the land, he also claimed that the colony's laws could not interfere in religious matters. Massachusetts authorities considered his views very dangerous. They decided that he was such a troublemaker that they banished him. By law he could never again set foot in Massachusetts.

Before he could be arrested, Williams and some of his followers fled from the colony. They went to live among the Native Americans in what was to become Rhode Island. Roger Williams won the trust of the Narragansett Indians. He learned to speak their language. They gave him title to land where he founded the town of Providence. Williams, in turn, served as a diplomat for the Narragansetts and helped them settle disputes both with the whites and with other Native Americans.

Roger Williams lived in this house in Salem, Massachusetts, before fleeing to Rhode Island.

*Providence became a safe place for people who held a variety of religious views to live and practice their religions. In 1638 Williams founded the first Baptist church in America. He continued to support himself by farming and trading while serving in various positions of leadership in Rhode Island. He died in Providence in 1683. Roger Williams is remembered as the founder of Rhode Island and the most important colonial leader who promoted religious freedom.*

Brass compass and sundial owned by Roger Williams

remained too close to the Church of England. His beliefs alarmed Massachusetts authorities. They considered him a dangerous man who threatened the basic beliefs that allowed Massachusetts to exist. In January 1636 Williams and a few followers fled across the colony's border on to land controlled by the Native Americans. Because he had previously earned the trust of the Narragansett leaders, they gave him the right to settle at the head of Narragansett Bay. Here Williams established Providence Plantation.

Providence was the first town that English colonists established in Rhode Island. The colonists cleared and fenced the land and made it a common, or shared ,property. They planted crops and raised cattle. They harvested nearby marsh grass to make hay and feed their livestock. They used marsh reeds to make thatch for their roofs. Over time, they built gristmills and sawmills along the Moshassuck River. The river's flow provided the power to work their machines. Between 1636 and 1640, Providence slowly grew to a population of about 100 people.

Providence enjoyed a unique form of government. All people were free to practice religion as they saw fit. At first the heads of the households met every two weeks to make political decisions. Later, the townspeople elected five people whose job was to listen to and resolve disputes. Providence's combination of religious tolerance and democracy made it a freer place to live than any other English colony.

### FROM ONE TOWN TO FOUR

Meanwhile, back in Boston, a new religious dispute erupted. A religious group emerged who called themselves Antinomians (the name means "against the law"). A stubborn and intelligent woman named Anne Hutchinson began to hold religious meetings for the Antinomians. She preached a radical religious doctrine based on the idea that all people had a direct relationship with God and had no need for ministers or church authority. This the Puritan authorities could not tolerate. In 1637 Antinomian leaders searched for a safe haven to practice their religion.

With the help of Roger Williams, the Antinomians purchased the island of Aquidneck from the Narragansetts. They renamed it Rhode Island and founded the town of Portsmouth. In 1638 after Anne Hutchinson was tried and

English farming scenes published in 1685. Rhode Island farmers used the same types of tools and worked in the same way. Beginning in upper left and moving clockwise: plowing; sowing; harrowing; fence building; treating a sick ox; driving a two-wheel cart; cutting grain with a sickle; harvesting with a scythe; making smoke to put the bees to sleep in order to harvest honey; transplanting a fruit tree.

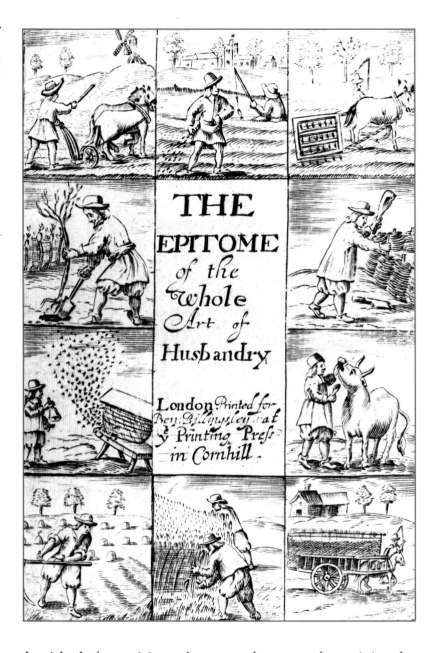

BANISH: TO EXPEL A CITIZEN FROM HIS OR HER COUNTRY

**banished** from Massachusetts, she moved to join the Antinomians in Rhode Island. The original colonists were a mixed group. They included farmers and servants, sailors and craftsmen. Among them were some wealthy merchants, including William Coddington, who hoped to make Portsmouth a prosperous commercial center.

Soon the people of Portsmouth began to feud over religious doctrines and how to govern themselves. So William Coddington led a splinter group across the island

Anne Hutchinson preaches in her Boston home.

to a place that had an excellent natural harbor. Here Coddington and his followers founded Newport. They divided up the land into large farms. Newport's most important leaders received so much land that they brought in additional people to farm the land.

By 1641 the people of Portsmouth and Newport came to the conclusion that they needed to cooperate in order to prosper. They joined together in a government that they described as "a democracy or popular government." They based the government on the right of **freemen** to make "just laws."

Among the men who settled in Newport was Samuel Gorton. Gorton was yet another religious troublemaker. Plymouth Colony had already expelled him. Even Roger Williams viewed Gorton with distrust. Gorton stirred up fresh troubles in Newport. He and his followers first moved to the town's outskirts and then, in 1643, across the bay to found the town of Warwick.

So it was that the English founded four major towns in Rhode Island: Providence, Portsmouth, Newport, and Warwick. All four were founded for the same reason: because of religion, the inhabitants could not live in harmony with other English people. At this time the people of the four Rhode Island towns neither liked one another nor anyone else and were distrusted by their neighbors in the adjacent colonies. Given these obstacles, it remained to be seen whether Rhode Island could create a successful colony.

**Above:** Nobody in Rhode island wanted the troublesome Samuel Gorton as a neighbor. Gorton and his followers purchased land from the Native Americans and built a new settlement.

In October 1643 Massachusetts authorities sent soldiers to arrest Gorton at his home in Warwick, supposedly for trespassing on land that Massachusetts claimed to control. After a two-day siege, they captured Gorton and his followers and marched them off in chains for trial. Gorton was found guilty not of trespassing, but of heresy. However, he and his followers were eventually freed and returned to Rhode Island.

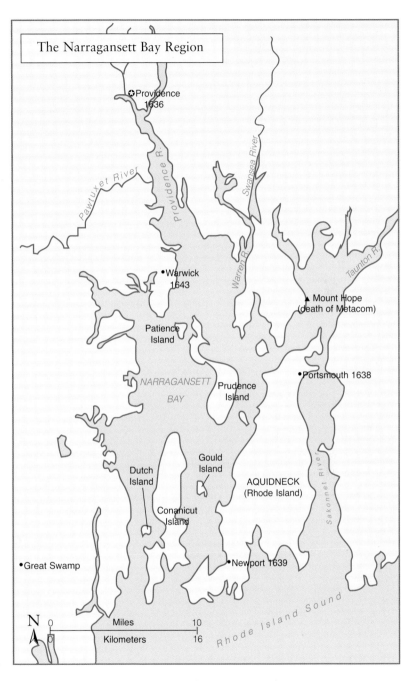

The Narragansett Bay Region

Providence 1636

Pawtuxet River

Providence R.

Swansea River

Warwick 1643

Warren R.

Taunton R.

▲ Mount Hope (death of Metacom)

Patience Island

• Portsmouth 1638

*NARRAGANSETT BAY*

Prudence Island

Gould Island

Dutch Island

AQUIDNECK (Rhode Island)

Sakonnet River

Conanicut Island

• Great Swamp

• Newport 1639

N

A

| Miles | 10 |

| Kilometers | 16 |

Rhode Island Sound

HERETIC: ONE WHO BELIEVES IN AN IDEA THAT HAS BEEN DENOUNCED AS A HERESY

Outsiders, particularly Massachusetts Puritans, considered the colonists in Rhode Island to be **heretics**, people who held false beliefs. At this time in history, being called a heretic often led to punishment and even death. Because Rhode Islanders were so different they were not invited to join the United Colonies, a military alliance of New England Puritan colonies that was created in 1643.

**CHARTER: A DOCUMENT CONTAINING THE RULES FOR RUNNING AN ORGANIZATION**

**PARLIAMENT: LEGISLATURE OF GREAT BRITAIN**

The Puritans often claimed that Rhode Islanders had no authority to govern themselves. To help secure the colony's future, Roger Williams returned to England in 1643. His goal was to obtain legal protection for Rhode Island from Parliament. William persuaded many powerful people that Rhode Island deserved protection. On March 24, 1644, Parliament granted Providence Plantation "a free and absolute Charter of Incorporation ... with full Power and Authority to rule themselves." Like all colonial **charter**s, laws had to conform "to the Laws of England." The charter of 1644 was important because it provided security at a time when the colony's neighbors were hostile. In addition, Providence now had the legal right of local self-government.

The granting of the charter did not change the nature of the Rhode Island people. They continued to argue. So it took three more years to agree about how to govern themselves. By 1647 the four towns agreed that each town could propose legislation. All towns had to be consulted before any law came into being. A general court would

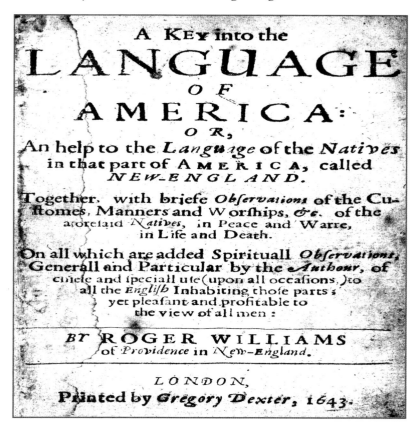

Williams' 1643 book, *A Key into the Language of America*, a guide to the Narragansett language and customs, impressed many powerful people in England and helped persuade them that Rhode Island deserved protection.

ASSEMBLY: LOWER HOUSE
OF A LEGISLATURE, WITH
DELEGATES ELECTED BY
THE VOTERS

assemble to pass laws. The basis of these laws was "the free and voluntary consent of all, or the greater part of, the free inhabitants." In between the meetings of the general court, a committee composed of six representatives from each town exercised political authority. By 1650 this committee became the colony's General **Assembly** or legislature.

The General Assembly ran the government. The colony's governor, its elected officials, and its courts all had to obey legislation passed by the General Assembly. Twice a year the colony's freemen elected members to serve in the General Assembly, and once a year they elected a governor. Because these elections took place so frequently, citizens had many opportunities to campaign, argue, and debate important issues.

The formation of a colonial government represented major progress. Still, during the entire seventeenth century, Rhode Island was an outcast among the English colonies. In the view of outsiders, Rhode Islanders followed faulty religious and political doctrines.

Roger Williams bringing home the Rhode Island charter of 1644. In 1663, King Charles II gave Rhode Island a new charter that continued the traditions of religious tolerance and self-government.

# 3.
# THE QUAKERS COME TO
# RHODE ISLAND

During the seventeenth century the Puritan movement became just one of many new religious sects. Some sects were so radical that they attracted few converts. Others were able to gain numerous converts, and the Society of Friends was one of these.

An Englishman named George Fox founded a new Christian religion, the Friends of God, or Society of Friends, around 1650. The Friends' beliefs, behavior, and appearance set them apart. Unlike other Christians, the

Friends did not have churches, worship services, or ministers. They held meetings in simple houses, and any person could speak at any time. They believed that each person had a direct relationship with God, and so did not need a minister to help communicate with him. People mockingly called the Friends "**Quakers**," because their founder said they should "quake" at the word of the Lord. However, the Friends did not at first call themselves "Quakers."

When members of the Society of Friends came to Massachusetts, Puritan authorities did not like it. The Massachusetts colony even executed four Quakers who had returned to the colony after being expelled. In 1656

Friends' meeting houses have a simple design and do not have steeples like churches do.

QUAKERS: MEMBERS OF THE SOCIETY OF FRIENDS, A CHRISTIAN GROUP FOUNDED IN ENGLAND AROUND 1650

A Quaker speaks to New Englanders in an effort to spread his religion.

Massachusetts banished Nicholas Upsall, a religious leader who had converted to Quakerism. Like so many others, Upsall came to Rhode Island to find religious freedom. Many of Upsall's followers joined him.

Similar incidents happened in the other colonies. For example, in 1657 the city of New Amsterdam (modern New York City) forbade a ship carrying Quakers from letting its passengers disembark. Two leaders of the Reformed Dutch Church, Johannes Megapolensis and Samuel Drisius, wrote that the Friends had probably sailed to Rhode Island "for that is the receptacle of all sorts of riff-raff people, and is nothing else than the sewer of New England. All the cranks of New England retire thither."

Samuel Gorton, the religious troublemaker who had founded Warwick, sympathized with the Quakers and invited them to Warwick. The Quakers soon gained more converts among the Rhode Islanders. Some of Newport's most influential men, including William Coddington, became Quakers. Quakers from all over New England came to Rhode Island to attend meetings. As time passed, the June meeting in Newport became the most important Quaker meeting of the year. Here the Quakers debated religious doctrines and figured out how to organize themselves throughout the colonies.

In the summer of 1672, Rhode Island Quakers received a big boost when George Fox, the founder of Quakerism, visited the colony. The Rhode Island Quakers became a well-organized and powerful political and economic force. Edmund Andros called them "the Quaker Grandees," in other words a rich ruling class. Perhaps as many as half of the colony's population belonged to the Society of Friends by 1690.

Tension, however, arose among religious thinkers in Rhode Island. In the summer of 1672 Williams debated three Quaker missionaries. The debate frustrated both sides. It was as if both sides made sense only to their own members. Yet Rhode Island managed to avoid the violence that often occurred elsewhere when people disagreed about religion. Roger Williams had founded the colony as a place of religious freedom. This freedom allowed the colony to endure without violent religious conflict.

A Quaker meeting. George Fox's journal lies on the table.

# 4.
## KING PHILIP'S WAR

In 1658 Rhode Island had only about 1,000 colonists. Although Rhode Island colonists tried harder than most to treat the Native Americans fairly, like other English colonists they too wanted more land. Roger Williams worked to protect the Native Americans from the English lust for land. He failed.

The powerful Narragansett people occupied most of the land. The Narragansetts were frequently at war with rival Native Americans. They also had fought against English colonists in Massachusetts and Connecticut. War and disease weakened the Narragansetts. Their leaders took to selling their lands to Rhode Island colonists in an effort to improve their situation. These sales allowed the Rhode Islanders to spread out from Narragansett Bay onto new territory.

In June 1675, war broke out between the Wampanoags and the English who lived in Massachusetts. The Wampanoags' leader was Metacom, or King Philip, as

New England settlers barricade their house against an Native American attack. In Rhode Island, attacks drove settlers from the mainland.

CONFEDERATION: LEAGUE OR UNION OF INDIVIDUALS OR GROUPS, SUCH AS TRIBES OR COLONIES, WHO WISH TO COOPERATE FOR ANY PURPOSE

MILITIA: GROUP OF CITIZENS NOT NORMALLY PART OF THE ARMY WHO JOIN TOGETHER TO DEFEND THEIR LAND IN AN EMERGENCY

the English called him. The New England **Confederation**, or United Colonies (all the English colonies in New England except Rhode Island) united to fight Metacom. Rhode Island was in an awkward position. Rhode Island leaders decided that they would not actively fight. However, they decided that Rhode Island ships could be used to move soldiers from outside the colony so that those soldiers could attack the Native Americans.

Although they had been enemies in the past, the Narragansetts joined Metacom's people and threw their entire strength into the fight against the whites. In December, the governor of Plymouth Colony, Josiah Winslow, led a combined force of New England **militia** and Native American allies in an attack against the Narragansetts. Rhode Island ships helped move the soldiers into position. Winslow entered Rhode Island and found the Narragansetts camped on high ground in the middle of a vast swamp. A bloody, day-long battle took place. The battle became known as "The Great Swamp Fight." The English lost 240 men killed and wounded, an enormous number for a battle in this era. But the Narragansetts suffered over 900 people killed and wounded. It was a terrible defeat for the Narragansetts.

Most of the important battles of the war took place in Massachusetts. Narragansett warriors left their families in Rhode Island in order to raid Massachusetts colonists.

The Great Swamp Fight took place in December 1675.

Among the English force that cornered Metacom were a few Rhode Island men.

However, from time to time the Narragansetts also raided in Rhode Island. The Native American threat caused colonists to abandon the town of Wickford. Even the old established towns around Narragansett Bay were not safe. The native peoples burned most of Warwick and attacked Providence. In spite of Roger Williams' appeals to spare the town, the Native Americans burned most of Providence including Williams' home. English refugees fled from the mainland to safety on Aquidneck (Rhode Island).

Connecticut soldiers and their Native American allies conducted brutal attacks against the Narragansetts. If they did not kill the Native Americans, they captured them and sold them into slavery. In August 1676, English soldiers cornered Metacom at Mount Hope, on the mainland east of Aquidneck. Among the English force were a handful of Rhode Island men. One of the allied Native Americans shot and killed Metacom. Metacom's death ended most Native American resistance.

King Philip's War, as the English colonists called it, was important for the history of Rhode Island. At first Rhode Island had only provided naval support to militia from the other colonies. Rhode Island authorities had allowed outside militia to enter the colony and hunt down the Narragansetts. Then while officials in Newport talked about peace, they permitted the execution of Native American captives and allowed others to be sold in slavery. By the end of the war, officials looked the other way while Rhode Island men actively fought the Native Americans.

By the time the war ended in 1676, many of the structures built by white settlers in Rhode Island had been destroyed. It took years for farmers to recover. The war reduced the Narragansetts from a powerful force to a weak group numbering only a few hundred people. The Narragansetts could no longer control their own lands. The English victors in Massachusetts, Connecticut, and Rhode Island competed to occupy the land that once had been the homeland of the Narragansetts.

# A Captive of the Native Americans

At sunrise on February 10, 1676, soon after the Great Swamp Fight, Narragansetts attacked and destroyed the town of Lancaster, Massachusetts. Wrote Mary Rowlandson, the wife of the town's Puritan minister, "Some in our house were fighting for their lives, others wallowing in their blood, the house on fire over our heads."

The attackers killed 12 men, women, and children and captured 24. Among those taken were Rowlandson and her three children. Rowlandson lived to write the story of her captivity, A Narrative of the Captivity and Restoration of Mrs. Mary Rowlandson, and it was published in Boston in 1682. Her youngest daughter was not so fortunate. Nine days after their capture, the badly wounded 6-year-old died.

As the houses burned and her friends and relatives fell, Rowlandson had faced a moment of truth: "I had often before this said, that if the Native Americans should come, I should choose rather to be killed by them than taken alive; but when it came to the trial my mind changed."

The Native Americans took Mrs. Rowlandson with them as they moved their village from place to place, covering some 150 miles (241 kilometers) of cold and rugged New England country. Rowlandson and her surviving two children, a girl of 10 and a boy of 14, were sold to separate owners among the Native Americans. A woman who had been captured along with Rowlandson talked about escaping and was tortured to death.

Mrs. Rowlandson, taking strength from her religious faith, survived. She met King Philip himself, and sewed some clothing for his son, for which he paid her. Other Native Americans then hired her to make clothing and paid her with extra food. Some Native Americans in the village treated her kindly: "If I went to their wigwam at any time, they would always give me something; and yet they were strangers that I never saw before." Others treated her spitefully, at times beating her or making her sleep outside, or telling her falsely that her son was dead and her husband remarried.

After eleven weeks of captivity among the Native Americans, Rowlandson was ransomed and released on May 3, 1676. Several months passed before her children were freed. Rowlandson's son was ransomed, and her daughter brought to Providence, Rhode Island, by a sympathetic Native American woman.

Mary Rowlandson's book sold well. It was the first of its kind, and stories of captivity among the Native Smericans became a popular form of American literature.

# 5.
# THE DOMINION OF NEW ENGLAND

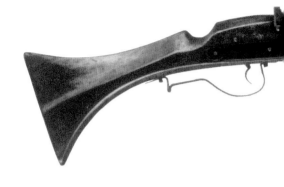

Compared to its English neighbors, Rhode Island remained weak. During the thirty years following King Philip's War, Rhode Island faced a difficult struggle to protect its borders against the ambitions of Massachusetts and Connecticut. It seemed that an independent Rhode Island was doomed when the English king, James II, ordered the establishment of the Dominion of New England. The king's idea was to create one large colony instead of numerous small ones in order to collect taxes more efficiently. Rhode Island became part of this dominion in 1687.

Governor Edmund Andros controlled the dominion from his offices in Boston. As time passed, resistance to Andros' rule sprang up. New Englanders objected to paying taxes unless their own representatives had voted for the taxes. Andros proved so unpopular that a group of armed civilians rebelled and captured him in 1689. Andros escaped from prison and fled to Newport. He probably expected that Newport would give him a safe place to live just like it did for religious refugees. Instead, Newport officials held Andros in jail until Massachusetts authorities came to get him. The arrest of Andros marked

This early matchlock musket was typical of the weapons used in the mid-1600s.

PRIVATEER: PRIVATELY-OWNED SHIP WITH GOVERNMENT PERMISSION TO ATTACK THE SHIPS OF ENEMY NATIONS DURING WARTIME

Opposite: Governor Andros walks in Boston.

the end of the Dominion of New England. Had the Dominion continued, tiny Rhode Island's larger neighbors almost certainly would have dominated the colony.

Although Rhode Islanders, in typical fashion, argued about how to govern themselves for years after the fall of Andros, the colony remained independent. By 1690, Rhode Islanders found, with difficulty, Henry Bull, a man willing to serve as governor of the argumentative colony.

Meanwhile, England and France went to war in 1689. The next year a fleet of seven French **privateers** attacked Block Island and threatened Newport. Governor Bull and his advisers organized a force including two ships to fight the French. A remarkable group provided the fighting force. They included "some seamen, leading citizens, Jews, a shipbuilder, white and Native American servants, and a doctor." Their leader was Thomas Paine, a retired pirate (no relation to the famous **patriot** with the same name).

Paine led his two-ship fleet against the French. A battle took place off the coast of Block Island. It lasted for several hours while worried islanders watched from the shore. There were no clear victors, yet to almost everyone's surprise, the French fleet sailed away the next day. During the remainder of the war the French attacked Block Island three more times, and succeeded in coming ashore twice.

Rhode Island leaders proved unable to organize the colony to fight the French. They quarreled among themselves and with Massachusetts leaders as well. Finally, they sought direction from royal authorities in London. In 1694 the English monarch, Queen Mary, sent a message to her subjects in Rhode Island about reorganizing the government. After many years of confusion, Rhode Island elected a government that could accomplish important tasks like raising a militia and collecting taxes. The single-house General Assembly was divided into a two-house legislature in order to satisfy the towns' demands for greater representation.

## 6.
# FARMERS AND SEAMEN

Like all North American colonists, Rhode Island's first white settlers had to produce enough food to feed themselves. The colony enjoyed some unique natural advantages that made this task easier. The waters of Narragansett Bay made the winters less severe. The islands, including Aquidneck (Rhode Island) itself, had about 5,000 acres of rich soil capable of supporting all sorts of crops. The islands had another 70,000 acres of decent soil suitable for some crops, apple orchards, and fine grazing. Most importantly, livestock grazing on the islands were safe from predators such as wolves. This fact allowed farmers to let their animals run free without

At the end of a day's work, colonial families continued working at home. In the evenings, they did such tasks as spinning thread or making clothing and other items.

Because hogs could fend for themselves better than sheep and cattle, raising hogs was especially popular.

having to worry about protecting them. In 1647 William Coddington noted that sheep flocks on Aquidneck doubled every year because of the absence of wolves.

Small farmers grew corn and hay and raised livestock. Because pigs could fend for themselves better than sheep and cattle, raising pigs was especially popular. When a farmer became better established, he planted apple orchards to make cider. Blessed by nature, the farmers prospered. As early as 1645 an English farming expert, Dr. Robert Child, described Rhode Island as a place full of "corn and cattle, especially sheep." The following year Edward Winslow of Plymouth said that the colony is "very fruitful and plentifully abounding with all manner of food."

Rhode Island agriculture allowed the colony to be self-sufficient in food. Small farmers could even produce enough to make a profit. Larger farms produced a **surplus**, particularly of livestock, that ships carried south and west along the coast to markets in Connecticut and New Amsterdam (later New York). Ships also traded with Boston. As time passed, farmers produced more, and so trading ships sought new markets. By 1649 Rhode Island cattle were being exported to Barbados in the West Indies.

Increased prosperity created a demand to connect Rhode Island with its neighbors. In 1640, at a town meeting in Portsmouth, townspeople chose a man to

SURPLUS: EXTRA

WEST INDIES: ISLANDS OF THE CARIBBEAN SEA, SO CALLED BECAUSE THE FIRST EUROPEAN VISITORS THOUGHT THEY WERE NEAR INDIA

In the 54 years after Roger Williams founded Providence, the colony had experienced remarkable economic progress. A writer declared in 1690 that the colony is "justly called 'The Garden of New England' for its Fertility and Pleasantness. It abounds with all Things necessary for the life of Man." This map shows the colony's boundaries in 1659.

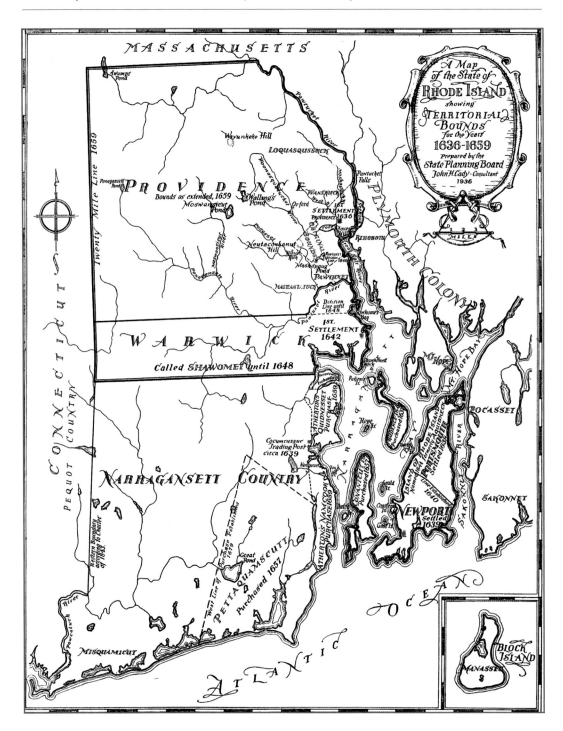

establish a ferry to cross the Sakonnet River. The ferry linked the island with the mainland. Soon there were more ferries operating all around Narragansett Bay. Next came road construction. The main New England road, the famous Post Road, ran from Boston to New York, passing through Rhode Island. Workers built roads from the ferries to join the Post Road. Drovers moved, or drove, livestock—hogs, cattle, sheep, and even horses—from Rhode Island to markets in Boston.

By 1690 Rhode Island's prosperous farms made enough money to pay for **imports** of European manufactured goods. Some farmers and merchants had enough profit to buy more land or invest in shipping. The wealthiest were able to afford imported luxury goods.

**Above:** Colonists bought colorful, decorative items for their homes as soon as they could afford them.

**Left:** A Puritan couple take a stroll.

During the best of times, farmers and merchants who exported agricultural goods could make enough money to live comfortably. Very few could become rich. So people sought other opportunities to make more money. Furthermore, Rhode Island had a limited amount of land suitable for farming. When there was no more land available to create new towns and farms, people turned to the sea. The colony's governor, Samuel Cranston, wrote in 1708 that the land "being all taken up and improved in small farms ... farmers, as their families increase, are compelled to put or place their children to trades or callings." The trade that most attracted young Rhode Islanders involved sailing ships.

Because of its excellent natural harbor, Newport became the colony's major seaport. By 1714 Newport had

Many fishing boats operated out of colonial New England ports.

A view of the colonial Rhode Island coast

grown to a population of about 2,200. The work of one in four Newport men revolved around the sea. Newport merchants established trading relationships all along the Atlantic coast and with merchants in the West Indies. At first, the major exports were livestock, timber products, and food. On their return voyages, Rhode Island ships carried manufactured goods as well as staples such as sugar, flour, rice, salt, and **molasses**, a byproduct of sugarcane, grown in the West Indies.

The import of molasses from the West Indies dramatically changed the colony's economics. Rhode Island distilleries used the molasses to make rum. Merchants sold the rum both to the local population and more importantly to towns all along the Atlantic coast from Canada to South Carolina.

Seaborne trade, particularly rum, allowed Rhode Island to prosper and grow. By the early 1730s, the colony's two major towns, Newport and Providence, had both doubled in size. The number of ships based in Rhode Island increased from 29 to about 80. Rhode Island sailors began crossing the Atlantic to Europe. The only problem with trading rum was that the profit was small. Then Rhode Island merchants discovered that they could make a great deal of money by entering the slave trade.

MOLASSES: DARK SYRUP PRODUCED WHEN SUGAR IS MADE FROM SUGAR CANE

## THE SLAVE TRADE

The Puritan religion taught that slavery was wrong except in the case of a captive taken in a just war. The colony's first slaves were Native American captives taken in the Pequot War during the 1630s. The Rhode Island general court said in 1652 that no black or white person should be held in bondage for longer than ten years. In other words, people regardless of race might be held as **indentured servants** for up to ten years and then set free. The first blacks came to Rhode Island as indentured servants.

In 1675 the general court passed a law that forbade making Native Americans slaves. Despite the colony's antislavery beliefs, many merchants thought there was nothing wrong with making money from trading in slaves.

INDENTURED SERVANT: PERSON WHO HAS AGREED TO WORK AS A SERVANT FOR A CERTAIN NUMBER OF YEARS IN EXCHANGE FOR FOOD, CLOTHING, A PLACE TO SLEEP, AND PAYMENT OF ONE'S PASSAGE ACROSS THE ATLANTIC TO THE COLONIES

The prosperous and growing town of Newport around 1730. The steeples represent a variety of Christian churches and meeting houses, including Anglican [Church of England] and Congregationalist.

So Rhode Island ships began to visit the West African coast to collect slaves. The ships delivered the slaves to the West Indies. There they picked up a cargo, the most important part of which was molasses. The ships brought the molasses to Rhode Island where most of it was distilled into rum. Americans, including Rhode Islanders, drank much of this rum. However, even more profit came from shipping the rum to Africa and trading it for slaves. This was one version of the so-called triangular trade: rum to Africa to trade for slaves; slaves to the West Indies where many of them worked on the sugar plantations; molasses to Rhode Island to be made into rum. Rhode Island's involvement in the triangular trade increased steadily until 1770. It was the most important business in the colony.

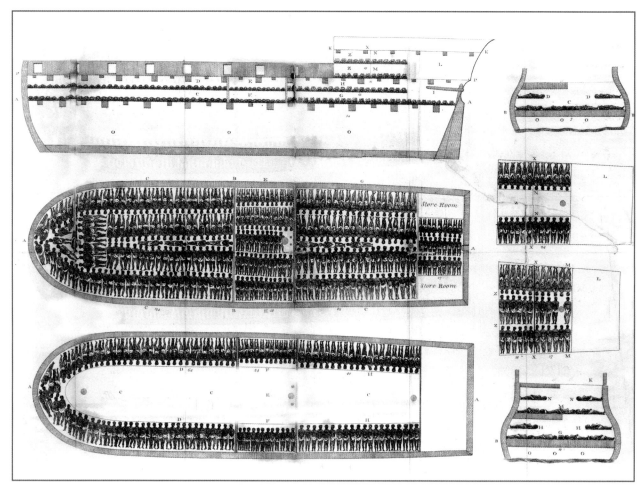

## GOVERNOR SAMUEL CRANSTON

Governor Samuel Cranston led Rhode Island for almost 29 years, from 1698 to 1727. During his time in office the colony changed from a loose cluster of villages into a prosperous colony. The key to the colony's well-being was Newport. Successful Newport merchants shipped Rhode Island products to ports around the Atlantic. Newport was Rhode Island's driving economic force. New roads were built in the colony's interior so that farm products could move more easily from farm to port. Merchants built new docks and wharves. Shipwrights constructed new vessels to add to the colony's growing merchant fleet.

Under Cranston's leadership, the colony enacted new laws to regulate trade. It even took the bold step of creating paper money so that merchants had an efficient means to conduct trade. Equally important, Cranston

African slaves are crammed aboard a slave ship. Traders packed in as many as they could on the African coast, expecting that a large number would die before they could be sold on the far side of the Atlantic Ocean.

PACIFIST: PERSON AGAINST WAR AND VIOLENCE; THE BELIEFS OF SUCH A PERSON

**Left:** A list of just some of the positions Samuel Cranston held shows his extraordinary public service: governor, president of the Council of War, chief judge of the Court of Trials, moderator of the Newport town meeting, presiding officer of the town council.

**Below:** The First Baptist Meeting House in Providence was completed in 1775. Roger Williams was one of the founders of America's first Baptist congregation.

worked to resolve border disputes with the neighboring colonies. He also successfully improved the colony's relationship with the English government while maintaining Rhode Island's independence.

Rhode Island's Quakers were **pacifists**. Nonetheless, Cranston successfully urged the colony to support England during the various wars against the French. The colony responded enthusiastically. News of Queen Anne's War reached Newport on June 25, 1702. In less than two weeks a Rhode Island warship went to sea to attack French ships in the Gulf of St. Lawrence. In 1708 and again in 1711, Rhode Island ships and men played active roles in the attacks against French possessions, including the invasion of Nova Scotia. Rhode Island's exploits pleased royal authorities in England.

## MORE RELIGIONS COME TO RHODE ISLAND

Several major religious movements swept New England during the 18th century. Because of its special attitude of tolerance, Rhode Island had a different experience from its neighbors.

**CONGREGATIONALIST:**
CHURCH ORGANIZED BY
PURITANS, BASED ON THE
IDEA THAT EACH
CONGREGATION GOVERNED
ITSELF WITHOUT
INTERFERENCE FROM A
CENTRAL AUTHORITY

**BAPTIST:** OFFSHOOT OF
PURIANISM BASED ON THE
BELIEF THAT ONLY ADULTS
CAN BE BAPTIZED, AND ON
LIMITING CHURCH
AUTHORITY OVER ITS
MEMBERS

Touro Synagogue, Newport, is the oldest synagogue in the United States and the only one still standing from colonial times. It was designed by Peter Harrison, an Anglican living in Newport.

Ministers representing the Church of England and **Congregationalists** (Puritans) were both able to preach in Rhode Island without opposition from either church or government authorities. The Great Awakening, a religious revival that swept through the colonies in the 1740s, did not create the same kind of excitement that took place elsewhere because Rhode Islanders were used to new religious ideas. The Great Awakening gave birth to new brands of religion including various types of Congregationalists and **Baptists.** Ministers representing both traditional and new religions tried to convert people in Rhode Island.

One religion that did not seek converts also blossomed in the tolerant soil of Rhode Island. A small congregation of Jewish people came from Brazil to Rhode Island around 1678. Although there were enough worshipers to hold services and purchase a cemetery plot, for unknown reasons this congregation did not thrive. A much larger influx of Jews came around 1750, many arriving from New York or the West Indies. Most lived in Newport. In 1754 they formed the Congregation Nephuse Israel (Scattered Ones of Israel). The Jewish population slowly increased so that they were able to dedicate the future nation's first synagogue in 1763. Like other Newport

merchants, Jewish merchants prospered and some entered into the colony's public affairs.

Aaron Lopez was the leading merchant. Lopez had a fleet of more than 30 trading vessels. Ezra Stiles, the pastor of the Second Congregational Church, wrote that Lopez was "a merchant of the first eminence, for honor and extent of commerce probably surpassed by no merchant in America."

## LIFE IN RHODE ISLAND IN THE 1700S

During the colony's early years, Native Americans dominated inland areas. Trees covered the land. English settlers huddled in small villages on Narragansett Bay's islands and shores, living in isolation from the neighboring colonies.

In imitation of wealthy people in Britain, wealthy Rhode Island merchants took to owning slaves to work as house servants.

Colonial life changed dramatically in the 1700s. After the Native American threat disappeared, increasing numbers of people moved inland. They cleared land and established new towns. Roads connected the towns. Ships crowded the bay, carrying Rhode Island agricultural products, molasses, and rum to ports along the Atlantic seaboard, the West Indies, Europe, and Africa. As time passed the colony managed to settle peacefully its boundary disputes with its bigger neighbors. Rhode Island enjoyed its position as a loyal and prosperous crown colony.

The way people lived depended on race, income, and sex. Most freemen were small farmers who also practiced a trade on a part-time basis. After Rhode Island merchants became involved in the slave trade, slavery spread within the colony itself. Shipowners allowed their captains to keep some of their slave cargo for themselves. Merchants wanted black people as house servants. The colony's largest farms, located in the southern part of Rhode Island, also relied on slave labor. In 1700 only about 300 black

Slaves worked on the large plantations in southern Rhode Island.

people lived among a white population of nearly 6,000. By 1774 the total population had grown about tenfold, and a black population of some 3,700 lived among a white population of almost 60,000.

In Newport, the colony's wealthiest town, most slaves worked as house servants. There, black servants outnumbered white servants eleven to one. On the Narragansett plantations in southern Rhode Island, black slaves worked to grow corn and tobacco and produce wool and dairy products. In Providence, some slaves worked as house servants while others labored for tradesmen.

Slave life in Rhode Island, particularly in the urban areas, was very different from slave life in the southern colonies. They were not as closely controlled. They freely associated with white workers who were in their same class. They drank in taverns alongside poor whites. They were encouraged to learn to read so they could read the Bible. Many had the same skills as free men.

Some slaves had the right to earn money and were sometimes able to purchase their freedom. A few masters

Above: Taverns and other shops displayed hand-painted wooden signs.

treated their slaves as indentured servants and set them free after they completed a term of work. Sometimes slaves ran away to find freedom. In these ways, a growing free black population emerged in Rhode Island. For example, among the 303 black people who lived in Providence in 1774, 46 lived in a household headed by a black person. Probably these fortunate 46 families lived as freemen. However, even free black people did not have the same privileges enjoyed by free whites.

During the time a white person labored as an indentured servant, his life was little different than that of a black slave. On Rhode Island's large plantations, white people worked alongside black workers performing the

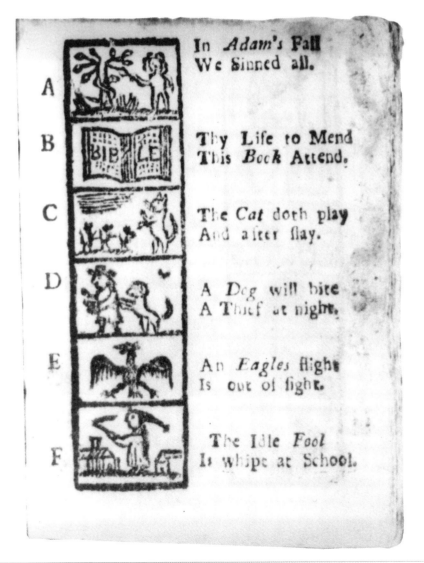

Right: A page from a 1727 New England reading primer

# Freeman / Apprentice / Indentured Servant / Slave

*In the colonies, a "freeman" was a free white man who possessed all the rights of citizenship, such as the right to vote, hold public office, or own land.*

*Colonial parents who did not have enough farm land to support their children, or lacked money to educate or train them in a useful occupation, sometimes bound their children as apprentices. Apprentices learned a craft or trade by working an agreed number of years for a master. Under some apprenticeship arrangements, the master was also responsible for teaching the apprentice to read and write. However, some masters got away with treating their apprentices poorly. At the end of the arrangement, the apprentice had a way to make a living, and sometimes continued to work for the master for a salary.*

*An indentured servant was a person who agreed to work as a servant for a certain number of years in exchange for food, clothing, a place to sleep, and payment of one's passage across the Atlantic to the colonies. At the end of the term of service, from four to seven years, the servant received clothing, tools, and sometimes land. Some masters treated their servants little better than slaves. Like slaves, servants could be bought and sold, and like slaves many performed the hardest labor in the colony. The law treated runaway servants harshly, and often permitted masters to discipline servants however they wished. Unlike slaves, when their indentures were over, servants became free. Still, the rest of society looked down on indentured servants.*

*Slaves were slaves for life, and their masters could treat them however they wished. In rare cases, a slave might be permitted to work for money and buy his freedom. Very few masters freed their slaves. Throughout the colonies, freed slaves did not have the same basic rights as free white people.*

Colonial women and men had different responsibilities at their homes and farms. Among their other chores, women cooked and served all meals.

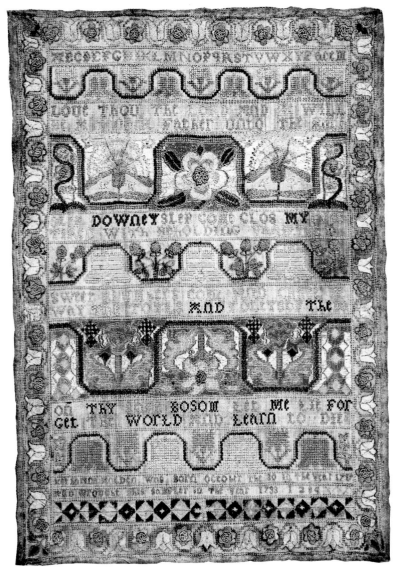

This sampler was made in Newport in 1733. Colonial women were responsible for making clothing. Girls practiced their sewing skills by making samplers.

APPRENTICE: PERSON WHO LEARNS A CRAFT OR TRADE BY WORKING FOR A MASTER

same chores. Indentured servants were bought and sold. For example, in Newport in 1761, two white women were convicted of theft. They could not pay their fine and instead were sold as indentured servants. Indentured servants were subject to harsh punishment at the whim of their masters. The *Providence Gazette* ran an ad in 1764 alerting people to look for an escaped eighteen-year-old apprentice. The boy had run away in order to avoid branding, the cruel punishment threatened by his master. Once indentured servants became free, they usually continued to occupy the lowest economic positions in the colony.

Many white people lived on the edge of poverty. In 1741 the Providence town council passed a law requiring the children of the poor to become apprentices for more wealthy tradesmen. If the male head of the household died, the poor widow faced a desperate situation. Town councils usually ordered her children to be taken as indentured servants. This meant that if she owned any land there was no one to work it. Often she would have to sell the land to pay for the basic necessities.

A woman's life in Rhode Island was very different from a man's life. Women worked to maintain the household. This meant they had to cook and clean, preserve food, spin, weave, sew, and wash the clothes. Few women managed to enter areas normally reserved for men, and those who ran their own businesses were exceptional. However, when male merchants died or went on long trading voyages, their wives often maintained the family business. Baptist and Quaker women participated fully in religious affairs, but women had no say in Anglican or Congregationalist churches.

# 7.
# A MATTER OF TAXES

A modern-day re-enactor dressed as a French soldier at the fortress of Louisbourg.

Great Britain fought a series of wars between 1739 and 1763. Until these wars, Rhode Island had been able to operate with a great deal of independence. During wartime, decisions made in London affected Rhode Island's prosperity. The wars forced the colony to cooperate more closely with the policies of the homeland. Many Rhode Islanders patriotically had supported Great Britain in its wars. Wealthy men fitted out warships to attack ships belonging to Britain's enemies. Others volunteered to serve aboard these ships. At the same time, merchants ignored some laws in order to trade with Britain's enemies.

Back in 1733 **Parliament** had passed the Molasses Act. This act made it illegal for New England to import molasses from the French West Indies to make rum. New Englanders ignored the Molasses Act and continued trade as usual even during the French and Indian War. General Jeffrey Amherst bitterly complained that Rhode Island merchants seemed interested only in making money regardless of whether this helped or hurt Great Britain.

After the French and Indian War ended in 1763, British leaders concluded that the American colonies had not helped as much as they should have. Moreover, the British government still needed to provide soldiers to defend the colonies. This was a heavy expense. Never before had the British Parliament set taxes on American citizens. This changed in 1764. To help pay for the cost of defending the colonies, Parliament passed the Sugar Act to raise money from the American colonies themselves.

The Sugar Act imposed a tax on imports and exports. Such taxes are called duties. The Sugar Act placed duties on refined sugar as well as other trade goods and provided for strict enforcement and collection procedures. The law greatly restricted Rhode Island's most profitable trade. It was the first in a series of decisions made by the British Parliament that eventually led to the American Revolution.

Next, in 1765 Parliament passed the Stamp Act. Under the Stamp Act, colonists had to pay to have most documents stamped, or risk arrest. Even newspapers had to have stamps. The Stamp Act affected colonists of all social classes. Resistance grew throughout the colonies. Riots broke out, and groups calling themselves the Sons of Liberty attacked the offices and homes of tax collectors. From the time of the Stamp Act until the outbreak of the Revolutionary War, conflict focused on the question of who had the right to impose taxes on the colonies.

Colonial leaders continued to protest what they considered unjust British rule, but they were against violence. Among the peaceful ways protesters opposed British laws was through the formation of Committees of Correspondence. By writing letters, the Committees kept one another informed and made plans for the colonies to cooperate. The Committees got all the colonies except New Hampshire to **boycott** English merchandise. The boycott convinced the British to repeal most taxes by 1770.

**Above:** Protest against the Stamp Act was widespread and took many forms. A teapot displays the words "No Stamp Act."

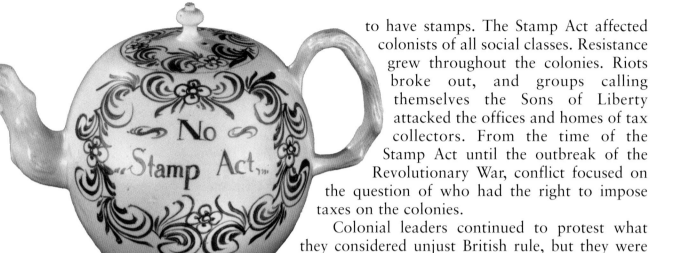

BOYCOTT: AGREEMENT TO
REFUSE TO BUY FROM OR
SELL TO CERTAIN
BUSINESSES

PATRIOTS: AMERICANS
WHO WANTED THE
COLONIES TO BE
INDEPENDENT OF GREAT
BRITAIN

SMUGGLING: SECRETLY
AND ILLEGALLY TRADING
IN FORBIDDEN
MERCHANDISE, OR HIDING
GOODS TO AVOID PAYING
TAXES ON THEM

Opposite bottom: A British
cartoonist made fun of the Stamp
Act by showing mournful British
officials holding a funeral for it after
it was repealed.

Below: The attack on the *Gaspee*

## 8.
# FROM BOYCOTT TO BATTLEFIELD

After 1770 **patriots** saw every action taken by the British government as a plot to take away American liberty. Nonetheless, Rhode Island prospered and colonial life remained calm until 1772. Few colonists really wanted independence from Great Britain, as long as they could make their own laws and set their own taxes. But Parliament continued to impose taxes. Among the taxes was a tax on tea. A Newport patriot warned, "By taxing ... tea [the British] will assume the same right to lay a tax on all you eat, drink, wear, and possess until you have nothing to be taxed for."

Many Rhode Island merchants responded to Parliament's taxes by turning to **smuggling** in order to avoid paying duties. These merchants thought that it was not wrong to evade a law when it had not been made by proper authority. The British government responded by trying to stop the smuggling.

Ships belonging to the Royal Navy patrolled the American coast to prevent smuggling. One of these ships was a schooner named the *Gaspee*. On the night of June 9, 1772, the *Gaspee* was chasing a smuggler in the waters of Narragansett Bay. Suddenly the *Gaspee* struck a shoal and ran aground. John Brown of Providence organized a party of men to attack the helpless British ship. A Rhode Island

The Boston Tea Party

sailor named Abraham Whipple led the attack. Whipple and his men burned the *Gaspee* and then escaped.

The British Prime Minister, Frederick North, created a Commission of Inquiry to investigate this unlawful act. A Royal Proclamation offered a reward for information. The Commission failed to uncover enough evidence to take Whipple and his men to trial. Rhode Island sailors, merchants, and smugglers celebrated the burning of the *Gaspee*. Most people in Britain viewed it differently. To them it was another example of lawlessness that was spreading throughout the American colonies.

LOYALIST: COLONIST WHO WANTED AMERICA TO REMAIN A COLONY OF GREAT BRITAIN

Rght: As early as 1756, Rhode Island Governor Stephen Hopkins asked, "What have the king and Parliament to do with making a law or laws to govern us by, any more than the Mohawks have?"

The next major act of lawlessness took place in nearby Boston. On December 16, 1773, a group of about 150 patriots dumped a valuable shipment of tea into Boston Harbor. Great Britain responded to the Boston Tea Party by closing the port of Boston and placing Massachusetts under military rule. The British goal was to teach all the colonies to submit to British rule. Patriots throughout the American colonies called the various British laws the Coercive Acts, or the Intolerable Acts. Increasing numbers of people argued that they would have to fight for independence from Great Britain.

Throughout the thirteen colonies, people debated about the proper relationship between America and Britain. Like the other colonies, Rhode Island was divided. The **loyalists**, or tories, were content to continue as British citizens. The rebels, or patriots, wanted to become independent of Britain. Rebels who wanted separation from Britain said that British leaders were violating the basic rights of the British people living in America.

The Rhode Island legislature set June 30, 1774, as a day of public fasting and prayer to protest the Intolerable Acts. Massachusetts patriots responded to the British actions more forcefully. They wanted to boycott British trade. They knew that the boycott had to involve all the colonies to be effective. They decided not to act until American leaders gathered in a congress of the colonies to discuss what to do.

The First Continental Congress took place in Philadelphia in September 1774. Stephen Hopkins and Samuel Ward served as Rhode Island delegates. Although the two men disagreed about many things, they agreed that the actions of the British **Parliament** and King were threats to Rhode Island's freedoms. The First Continental Congress drew up a set of resolutions. These resolutions set forth basic rights to life, liberty, property, and the rights of colonial assemblies to tax and make local law. The delegates agreed to end all imports from Great

Britain in order to pressure Parliament to accept their views. They formed a Continental Association by which every village, town, and city was to elect a committee to enforce the decrees of the Continental Congress.

The First Continental Congress moved the American quarrel with Great Britain beyond just taxes. In addition to tax questions, the congress questioned whether Parliament had the right to make laws for America. The delegates agreed to meet again in May 1775.

The Rhode Island Assembly enthusiastically agreed with the actions taken by the First Continental Congress. It created local Committees of Inspection to make sure that everyone boycotted British goods. When anyone cooperated with the British, he was severely criticized in the papers. For example, a man who sold sheep to a British warship was named in Rhode Island newspapers as an enemy to his country. By shaming people who expressed pro-British views, Rhode Island increasingly became more inclined to support revolution.

The General Assembly also changed the colony's militia laws so that Rhode Island men could march to assist the neighboring colonies. The Assembly resolved to raise a force of 1,500 men. When the governor objected, the assembly expelled him from office. The *Newport Mercury* proudly wrote in November 1774 that there was "a martial spirit running through the country."

## THE REVOLUTION BEGINS

After the fighting began at Lexington and Concord, Massachusetts, on April 19, 1775, Rhode Island militia participated in the seige of Boston. On May 4, 1776, the General Assembly voted to end the colony's allegiance to King George III because he had departed "from the duties and character of a good king." The Assembly charged that King George III was trying "to destroy the good people of this colony, and of all the United Colonies, by sending fleets and armies to America." The Assembly agreed that Rhode Island must resist the king's tyranny with all its strength. Two Rhode Island delegates to the Continental Congress, William Ellery and Stephen Hopkins, signed the Declaration of Independence. On July 18, 1776,

William Ellery, one of the two Rhode Islanders who signed the Declaration of Independence, attended the Continental Congress in the place of Samuel Ward, who had recently died. Stephen Hopkins was the other signer.

Left: Esek Hopkins of Rhode Island, the brother of Stephen Hopkins, became the first commander in chief of the Continental Navy.

**Above:** The French general, Comte [Count] de Rochambeau.

**Below:** The Rhode Island general, Nathanael Greene, was one of the most successful American leaders during the Revolutionary War. He was born to Quaker parents in Rhode Island in 1742.

the colony approved the Declaration of Independence and declared itself the independent State of Rhode Island and Providence Plantations.

During the Revolutionary War, Rhode Island was the scene of many raids and battles on both land and sea. The state raised five regiments including the excellent Second Rhode Island Regiment, whose ranks included many black men. Warships set out from Narragansett Bay to raid British shipping. The British occupied Newport in December 1776 and stayed there until October 1779. During the British occupation, loyalists formed their own unit.

Three times rebel forces tried to drive the British from Rhode Island. The third time, in August 1778, a large French force helped. All three efforts failed. After the British decided to leave Newport, in 1780 the Count de Rochambeau and his French army as well as a French fleet began using Newport as a base. In 1781 Rochambeau began his historic march from Newport to Yorktown, Virginia, where the combined American and French army captured Cornwallis's British army.

# EPILOGUE

In 1787 Rhode Island's General Assembly voted for the gradual freeing of black slaves.

Three years later, on May 29, 1790, Rhode Island approved the United State Constitution and became the 13th state. It was the last of the original 13 colonies to approve the Constitution because it waited until the Bill of Rights was added.

Modern Rhode Island has the smallest land area of any state and a population of slightly more than one millon. However, it is the second most densely populated state after New Jersey. Less than 4% of Rhode Island's population is black. A few thousand Narragansetts and Wampanoags still live in Rhode Island.

Nine out of ten people live in cities, the largest of which are the capital, Providence, followed by Warwick, Cranston, and Pawtucket. Forests have grown back on more than half of Rhode Island's land, much of which had been farmed in colonial times.

Only about 1% of Rhode Island's economy is based on agriculture. The major farm products include trees, shrubs, and sod for landscaping. About a third of the workforce is involved in manufacturing such products as textiles, plastic goods, machinery, electronics, jewelry, and

silverware. American textile manufacturing had its beginnings at Slater Mill at Pawtucket in 1790. Naval bases, ship builders, and fishing fleets also operate along Rhode Island's coast.

Rhode Island attracts visitors to its beaches and boating centers, as well as to Newport's famous music festivals. The original settlement of Providence, now a modern capital city, still has a neighborhood of carefully restored colonial buildings. The Roger Williams National Memorial marks the site where Providence began. Visitors can also see the General Nathanael Greene Homestead. The prominent Revolutionary War general from Rhode Island took part in battles in New Jersey and in North and South Carolina. He built the house in Coventry in 1770.

An early view of the college, built in Providence in 1770, that eventually became Brown University. The large building served as a barracks and hospital during the American Revolution.

# DATELINE

**1524:** Giovanni da Verrazano explores the coast of New England.

**1614:** Dutch explorer Adriaen Block maps the Rhode Island coast.

**1620:** The Pilgrims establish Plymouth Colony in Massachusetts.

**1629:** The Puritans found Massachusetts Bay Colony.

**1631:** Roger Williams travels from England to Boston.

**1635:** Roger Williams is banished from Massachusetts for his beliefs. He leads his followers to Rhode Island early the next year and founds Providence.

**1638:** Anne Hutchinson and her followers, banished from Massachusetts for their beliefs, move to Rhode Island.

**MARCH 24, 1644:** England's Parliament grants Rhode Island a charter allowing it to govern itself.

**1675–1676:** King Philip's War, between the colonists and the Wampanoag Indians, results in the Native Americans' defeat and the death of their chief, Metacom.

**1687–1689:** Rhode Island is forced to be part of the Dominion of New England.

**1690:** A French fleet attacks Block Island and is driven off by two Rhode Island ships.

**1754:** Jews form a congregation in Newport. They build the nation's first synagogue, completed in 1763.

**JUNE 9, 1772:** The *Gaspee*, a British ship patrolling for smugglers, runs aground off Providence. Local merchants attack and burn the vessel to the water line, after first evacuating all the sailors. The attackers go unpunished.

**JULY 18, 1776:** Rhode Island declares itself the independent State of Rhode Island and Providence Plantations.

**DECEMBER 1776–OCTOBER 1779:** British troops occupy Newport.

**1780–1781:** The French commander, Rochambeau, uses Newport as a base for assisting the Americans.

**MAY 29, 1790:** Rhode Island becomes the last of the thirteen colonies to accept the United States Constitution.

# GLOSSARY

ANGLICAN: Church of England, a Protestant church and the state church of England

APPRENTICE: person who learns a craft or trade by working for a master

ASSEMBLY: lower house of a legislature, with delegates elected by the voters

BANISH: to expel a citizen from his or her country

BAPTIST: offshoot of Puritanism, based on the belief that only adults can be baptized, and on limiting church authority over its members

BOYCOTT: agreement to refuse to buy from or sell to certain businesses

CHARTER: document containing the rules for running an organization

CONFEDERACY / CONFEDERATION: league or union of individuals or groups, such as tribes or colonies, who wish to cooperate for any purpose

CONGREGATIONALIST: church organized by Puritans, based on the idea that each congregation governed itself without interference from a central authority

DUTY: tax collected on goods brought into a country

EPIDEMIC: widespread outbreak of contagious disease

EXPORT: to send merchandise out of the country for sale; merchandise sent out of the country

FREEMAN: free white man who possessed all the rights of citizenship, such as the right to vote, hold public office, or own land

GLACIER: large area of ice and snow that expands during an "ice age," and reshapes the land by pushing soil and rocks from one place to another

HERESY: belief that is denounced by one's church

HERETIC: one who believes in an idea that has been denounced as a heresy

IMPORT: to bring merchandise into the country for sale; merchandise brought into the country

INDENTURED SERVANT: person who has agreed to work as a servant for a certain number of years in exchange for food, clothing, a place to sleep, and payment of one's passage across the Atlantic to the colonies

LOYALIST: colonist who wanted America to remain a colony of Great Britain

MILITIA: group of citizens not normally part of the army who join together to defend their land in an emergency

MOLASSES: dark syrup produced when sugar is made from sugar cane

PACIFIST: person against war and violence; the beliefs of such a person

PARLIAMENT: legislature of Great Britain

PATRIOTS: Americans who wanted the colonies to be independent of Great Britain

PRIVATEER: privately-owned ship with government permission to attack the ships of enemy nations during wartime

PROTESTANT: any Christian church that has broken from away from Roman Catholic or Eastern Orthodox control

PURITANS: Protestants who wanted the Church of England to practice a more "pure" form of Christianity

QUAKERS: members of the Society of Friends, a Christian group founded in England around 1650

RADICAL: holding beliefs that are extremely different from those of the majority; believing in the need for major changes in society

SASSAFRAS: type of tree whose bark is used for flavoring and medicinal purposes

SMUGGLING: secretly and illegally trading in forbidden merchandise, or hiding goods to avoid paying taxes on them

SURPLUS: extra

WEST INDIES: islands of the Caribbean Sea, so called because the first European visitors thought they were near India

## FURTHER READING

Brenner, Barbara. *If You Were There in 1776.* New York: Bradbury Press, 1994.

Smith, Carter, ed. *Battles in a New Land: A Source Book on Colonial America.* Brookfield, Conn.: Millbrook Press, 1991.

Smith, Carter, ed. *The Revolutionary War: A Source Book on Colonial America.* Brookfield, Conn.: Millbrook Press, 1991.

Wilbur, C. Keith. *The New England Indians.* Chester, Conn.: Globe Pequot Press, 1990.

## WEBSITES

http://www.americaslibrary.gov
Select "Jump back in time" for links to history activities

http://www.narragansett-tribe.org

http://www.thinkquest.org/library/JR_index.html
Find links to numerous student-designed sites about American colonial history

**Disclaimer**

All the Internet addresses (URLs) given in this book were valid at the time of going to press. However, due to the dynamic nature of the Internet, some addresses may have changed, or sites may have changed or ceased to exist since publication. While the author and publishers regret any inconvenience this may cause readers, no responsibility for any such changes can be accepted by either the author or the publishers.

## BIBLIOGRAPHY

Bridebaugh, Carl. *Fat Mutton and Liberty of Conscience: Society in Rhode Island, 1636–1690*. Providence: Brown University Press, 1974.

Cottrol, Robert. *The Afro-Yankees: Providence's Black Community in the Antebellum Era*. Westport, Conn.: Greenwood Press, 1982.

Coughtry, Jay. *The Notorious Triangle: Rhode Island and the African Slave Trade, 1700–1807*. Philadelphia: Temple University Press, 1781.

Crane, Elaine Forman. *A Dependent People: Newport, Rhode Island, in the Revolutionary Era*. New York: Fordham University Press, 1985.

James, Sydney V. *Colonial Rhode Island: A History*. New York: Charles Scribner's Sons, 1975.

Middleton, Richard. *Colonial America: A History, 1607–1760*. Cambridge, Mass.: Blackwell, 1992.

Salisbury, Neal, ed. *A Narrative of the Captivity and Restoration of Mrs. Mary Rowlandson*. Boston: Bedford/St. Martins, 1997.

Taylor, Alan. *American Colonies*. New York: Viking, 2001.

*The American Heritage History of the Thirteen Colonies*. New York: American Heritage Publishing Co., 1967.

# INDEX